A MAP BACK TO ME

Dear Angela
Thank you
for all you
do and trusting in me
Enjoy!
Jane x.

JANE SILVER

Book Design by HMDPublishing.com

ABOUT THE BOOK

This poetry book is for those who have trusted me enough with their stories, enabling me to find inspiration and creativity and in doing so, helping them to understand how to find their maps.

"A Map Back to Me" enables the reader to connect inwards to find a way through the blocks rather than getting stuck.

Each poem brings something new and different to life and connects psychology, neuroscience, energy healing, and soma-tics into an easy-to-read formula that can be used in an educational setting or for enjoyment. Poetry is so important in fostering creativity, building emotional intelligence and empathy helping to build self-awareness and a global understanding.

Enjoy!

Jane

ABOUT THE AUTHOR

Jane started life as as secretary working in a small Unit based at the University of Manchester and spent the next 17 years working with the Director of Human Resources.

He saw something in her that made him send her back to college one day and one evening per week to study CIPD. (Professional human resource management examinations). She moved departments to work with medical students in their representative council, where she worked with students around pastoral care and advice gaining the trust of all whom she worked with on both personal and student matters.

It was there she realised that 'helping people to solve their problems' was what she loved and after seven happy years, took herself back to studying counselling & therapeutic techniques, including counselling and hypnotherapy, counselling and psychotherapy, neurolinguistic programming, psychometric analysis, mindfulness, cognitive behavioural therapy, emotional freedom technique and gestalt therapy.

This culminated in her completing ILM level 7 (master's level equivalent) in Life and Business Coaching Leadership, Management, Mentoring and Mediation.

In 2010 she opened the doors to a private integrative counselling practice where she now fuses "NICE" guideline therapeutic techniques with the many new and innovative holistic modalities available. Her practice continues to go from strength to strength with clients coming from all over the World.

She is the author of "It'sToo Hard to Be Perfect" and has an on-line course launching soon.

CONTENTS

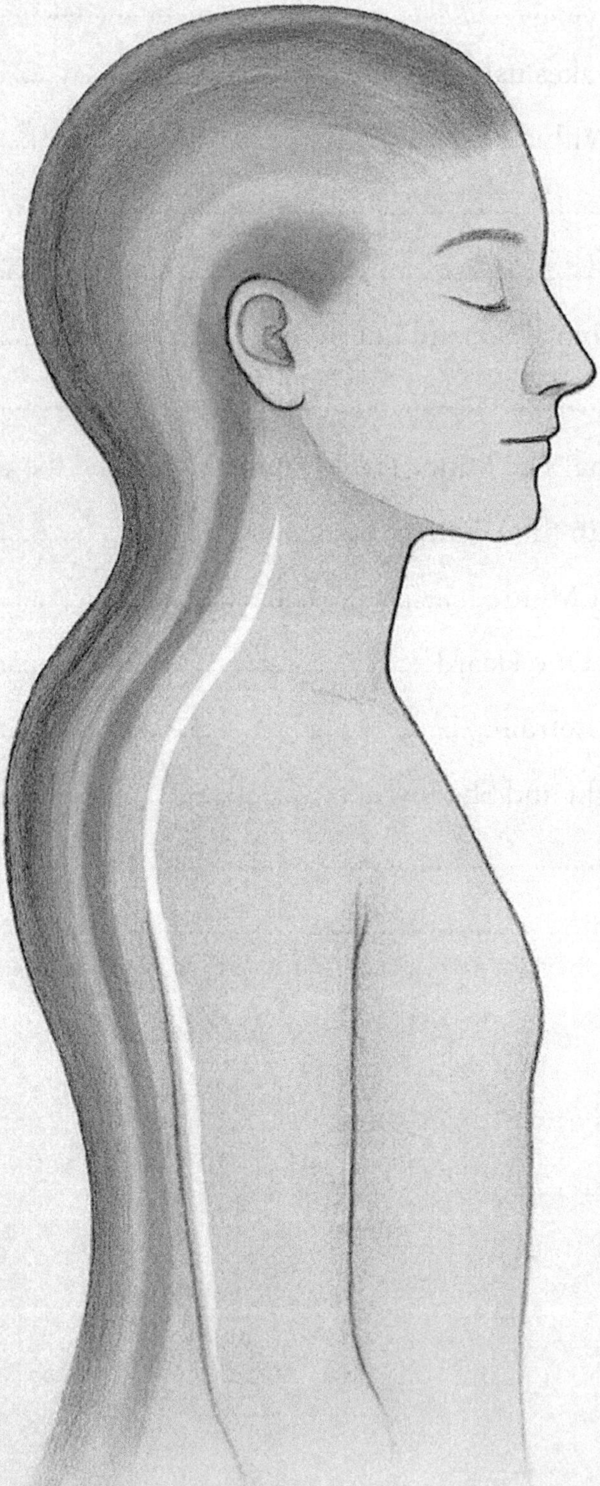

The Rainbow of Colour

The rainbow of colour can teach us a lot, but first we must learn to connect each pot.

Red brings freedom from struggle and pain, while orange brings nurture, like soft summer rain. Yellow restores us, calm in our core, and green helps us open, connect, and explore.

Blue is for healing, like sky wide and true, no need for the questions, just trust what is you.

Indigo deepens the way that we see, and violet brings balance, to simply be free.

The body speaks clearly, in colours and tone, a language of energy, all on its own. Emotions can block us, make systems feel tight, but colour can gently return us to light.

So, tune into each shade, let your feelings decide, from root up to crown, let your energy glide. When all flows with ease, from your head to your toes, you live in alignment and your true self glows.

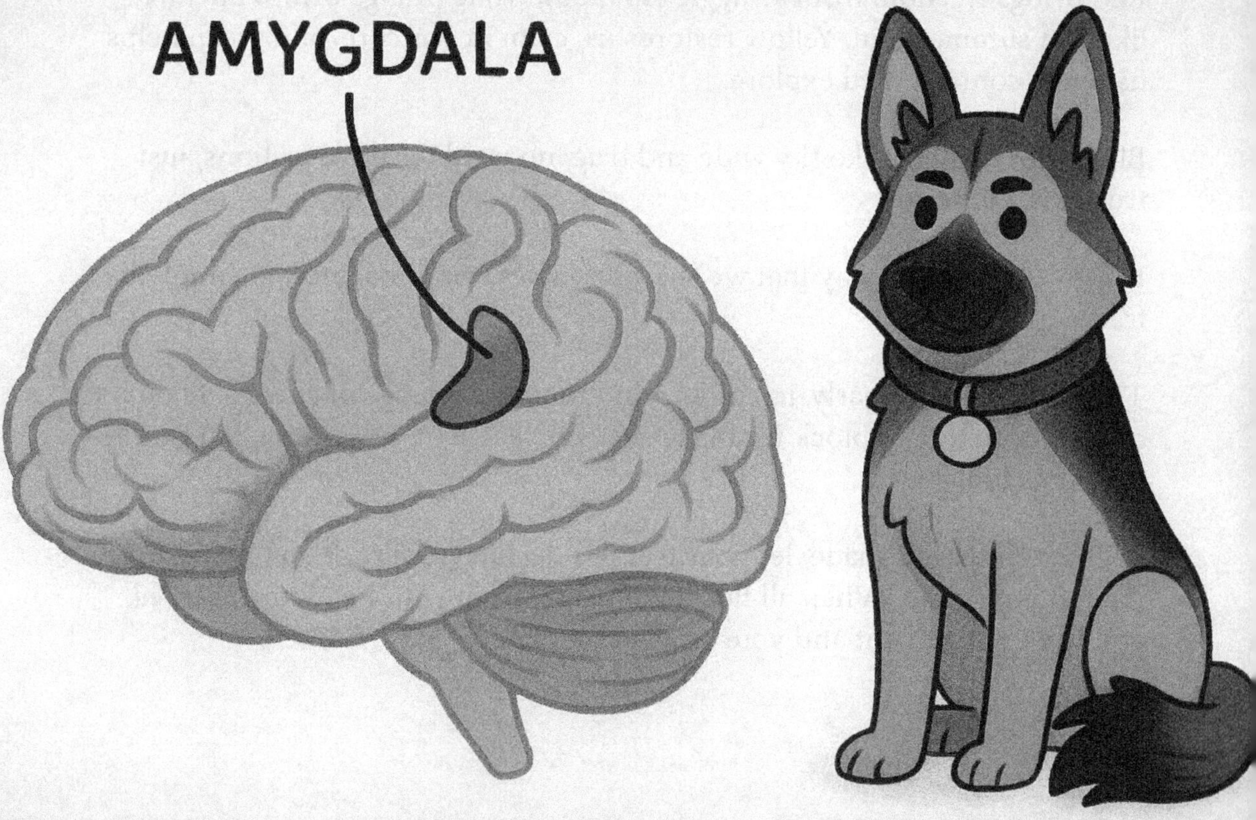
AMYGDALA

Amygdala

Deep in your brain lives a watchdog bold, the amygdala tiny, but quick to scold. It barks at a sound, a glare, or a glance, and throws your cool brain in a panic dance!

It doesn't ask questions, it doesn't play fair, it just shouts, "Danger!" and fills you with scare. Before your smart brain can say, "Hold tight," you're yelling or freezing or ready to fight.

See, signals take two roads in your head, one's nice and slow, the other's full speed ahead. The fast one zooms to your emotional pup, who sounds the alarm and gets fired up.

The slow road leads to the thinking zone, where logic lives and calm is grown. But by the time it gets there, oops! Too late, the watchdogs already slammed the gate.

This amygdala hijack steals your cool, and makes you bark, or cry, or duel. But here's the trick you're not stuck that way, you can teach that pup to sit and stay.

Take a breath, stretch your toes, splash your face or strike a pose. The vagus nerve that magic wire can cool the brain and quench the fire.

With mindful moves and moments slow, you tell your watchdog, Easy, bro! And bit by bit, you gain control, bringing peace back to your soul.

The Gentle Reset

When feelings are heavy and thoughts start to race, and your body's reacting but can't find a place. There's a reason you're stuck, though you try to let go, it's your brain and your body both saying "No."

Deep in your brain is a part called the "Amyg," it keeps you alert when life feels too big. It watches for danger, both real and not there, and sends out alarms to say, hey beware!

When triggers arise, it can panic or freeze, keeping stress in your system like a locked-up disease. Now science has shown what we long felt was true, emotions live in the body, not just thoughts in you.

They're patterns and pathways, like loops on repeat. Wired by memories some bitter, some sweet. But here comes a tool that is gentle and wise, it taps on your skin while you close your eyes.

You focus on feelings, the fear or the shame, while tapping sends signals to soothe the brain. Those acupoints tapped are no mystical show, they calm down the circuits that shout out go!

They light up receptors that speak to your mind, saying breathe, you are safe, leave the fear behind.

The cortisol drops, the heart finds its beat, and suddenly tension flows out through your feet. The pathways once wired in panic and pain can now be rewired through tapping the brain.

You're not just pretending or pushing it down, you're facing the storm without letting it drown. It's science and soul in a dance well-aligned, a therapy grounded, yet deeply kind.

So, if you're overloaded, stuck, or feel strange, remember your system is wired for change. With fingers that tap, and a phrase said with grace, you're giving your brain a much calmer place.

Not magic, but healing, from body to thought, with neuroscience guiding the wisdom you've sought. Your energy flows and your nervousness fades, as old fears dissolve and new peace invades.

TAPPING POINTS

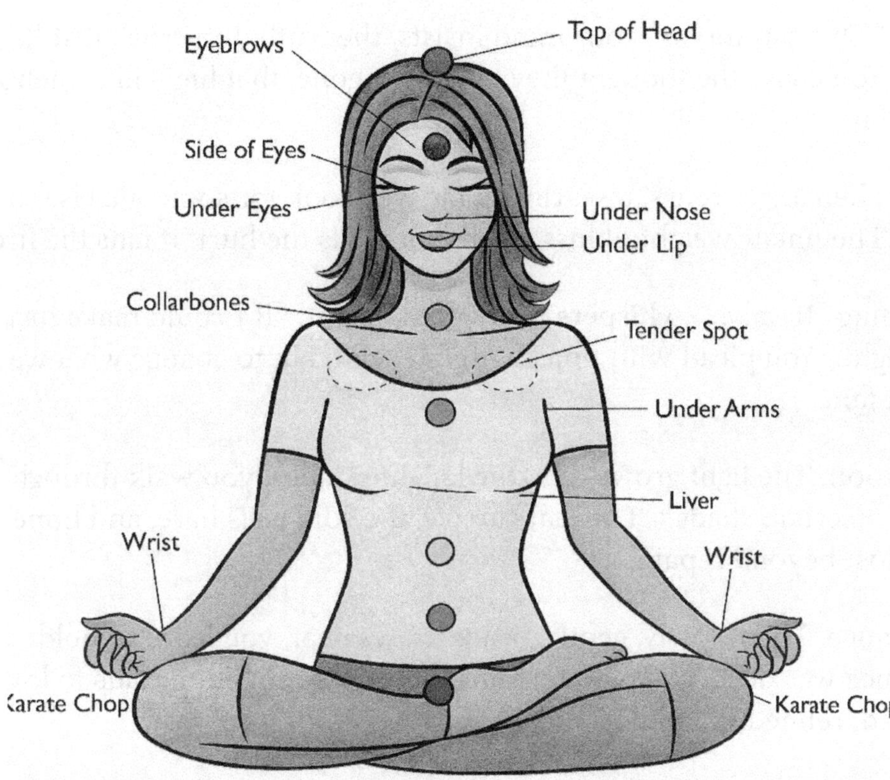

Remember to Breathe

The Stages of Grief

Shock. The world stands still, the sound is gone, you blink but life keeps moving on. Your breath is short, your heartbeat loud, you drift apart from time and crowd.

Denial "This cannot be," your mind insists, the truth, too cruel, it still resists. You chase the thought they're not yet gone, that life will somehow just go on.

Anger. Then anger roars, a searing flame, you look for someone else to blame. The unfair weight of loss, so dire, it feeds the hurt, it fans the fire.

Bargaining "If only..." whispers through the night, "If I could make just one thing right." You plead with time, with fate, with air, to change what was to make it fair.

Depression. The light grows dim, the laughter fades, you walk through grief's uncertain shades. The tears arrive, the soul feels bare, and hope seems lost beyond repair.

Acceptance. Then slowly, gently, peace draws near, you learn to hold what once was dear. The pain remains, but less confined, It folds to love, reshaped, refined.

Beyond. For love transcends both space and breath, it lingers still, defying death. Though hearts may break, they also mend, in grief begins where love won't end.

A Maze Through Therapy

Art therapy paints what words can't show, through colour and clay, emotions flow.

Behavioural therapy teaches anew, to unlearn fears, and choose what's true.

Coaching helps your strengths take flight and guides your goals toward the light.

Cognitive therapies, wise and keen, help shift the way our thoughts are seen.

CBT blends thinking and doing, for brighter moods and better viewing.

Creative therapy breaks the wall, through dance or drama, we recall.

Eclectic minds mix what they know, to tailor healing as you grow.

Emotionally focused hearts entwine; it helps love's bonds again align.

Existential asks the soul, what gives your life its meaning, whole.

EMDR moves eyes in sleep's own trance, to heal the past, to give peace a chance.

Family therapy mends the thread, between what's spoken and unsaid.

Gestalt says, here and now, let us see, what is, truly felt by you and me.

Humanistic shines its rays, on self-growth's path through honest gaze.

Integrative therapy blends each part mind, body, soul, and open heart.

IFS within us finds, the parts made whole as self aligns.

Interpersonal mends ties that ache, Jungian therapy dreams awake.

Narrative says, rewrite your tale, you are not the storm or gale.

NLP reprograms the mind, to shape new habits, more aligned.

Person-centred sits with care, unconditional love laid bare.

Phenomenological asks what's true? Let's see the world from your own view.

Play therapy lets children show, through games, the feelings they can't know.

Primal revisits pain so deep, to wake the wounds from ancient sleep.

Psychoanalysis dives below, where dreams and memories still flow.

Psychodynamic takes that stream and brings insight into the dream.

Psychosynthesis lifts the soul, unites the parts to make you whole.

Relationship therapy steadies the air, when love feels lost, it teaches care.

Solution-focused, short and sweet, helps you find where strengths and goals meet. Systemic sees how bonds entwine, and how one shift can realign.

Transactional analysis helps us see, the parent, adult, and child in me. Transpersonal therapy softly calls, beyond the self, where spirit sprawls, it blends the human and divine, where healing hearts and souls align.

So many ways to talk, to feel, to paint, to move, to love, to heal. Each therapy a gentle art, a mirror held to mind and heart.

A Poetic Tour of the Twelve Cranial Nerves

Cranial Nerve One, the Olfactory's call, it carries the fragrance of flowers, smell most of all.

Cranial Nerve Two, the Optic in line, it gathers the light, so your vision is fine.

Cranial Nerve Three, the Oculomotor, it opens your eyelids, adjusts pupils' border.

Cranial Nerve Four, the Trochlear so neat, It helps point your eyes down, or inward to meet.

Cranial Nerve Five, the Trigeminals might, brings touch to your face and lets chewing feel right.

Cranial Nerve Six, the Abducens will glide, it moves your eyes outward, from side to side.

Cranial Nerve Seven, the facial with flair, it smiles and it frowns, taste buds join it there.

Cranial Nerve Eight, Vestibulocochlear sings, it balances bodies and hears when bell rings.

Cranial Nerve Nine, the Glossopharyngeal true, Helps swallow, makes saliva, tastes flavours too.

Cranial Nerve Ten, the Vagus so vast, it slows down your heartbeat, keeps breathing steadfast.

Cranial Nerve Eleven, Accessory's role, It shrugs up the shoulders and steadies the pole.

Cranial Nerve Twelve, the Hypoglossal strong, It wiggles the tongue for both speech and for song.

THE LANGUAGE OF THE MIND

Some see the world in colours bright, with pictures, patterns, shapes in sight. If visions guide the path you take, you're visual learning wide awake.

Some hear the world through song and sound, in rhythm, voices all around. If tone and talk help you to know, auditory is how you grow.

Some count on words inside the head, thoughts ticking, talking, neatly said. If logic, labels lead you through, auditory digital speaks for you.

Some feel the world in touch and ground, in heart, in movement, safe and sound. if body, senses, hold your key, Kinaesthetic's your energy.

There is no best, no right, no wrong, each system sings its vital song. When you know yours, the world turns clear, your way of learning will appear.

It's Too Hard to Be Perfect

We chase the stars, we climb so high, we fear the fall, we fear the sky. We polish masks until they shine, pretending all is smooth, divine.

But cracks will show, they always do, for flaws are proof that we are true.

Perfection's weight is sharp and cold, a story tired, forever told. It whispers lies of who we should be, hides tender truths we cannot see.

It covers fear, it hides the scar, It tells us we're not good as we are. Yet life is richer when it's real, when messy hearts can laugh and feel.

Mistakes are teachers, not disgrace, they give our souls their truest face. So let the mask slip, let it fall, you're more than perfect after all.

For perfect is a fleeting art, but honest living heals the heart.

The Feelings Wheel

At the center lies a simple start, emotions beating from the heart. Joy, anger, sadness, fear, surprise, disgust the core is clear.

Like branches stretching from a tree, these roots expand so we can see. Joy may blossom into pride, or peaceful calm we hold inside.

Sadness grows to grief or shame, each subtle shade with its own name. Fear might swell to nervous doubt, or anxious thoughts that circle out.

The wheel reminds us, look within, name the place where you have been. For when you find the word that's true, you'll know just what your heart tells you.

It's not to judge or push away, but guide your feelings day by day. A map for minds, both young and wise, a compass where our meaning lies.

So spin the wheel, explore, reveal, the layers of the way you feel. For every word brings gentle light, to turn confusion into insight.

The Five Basics of Mindfulness

Set intention, calm and bright, like a compass, day and night.
Attention lands on breath, on now, the present moment shows you how.

Acceptance says, just let it be, a flowing tide, wild yet free.
Non-judgment clears the heavy load, no right, no wrong, just walk the road.

Connection grows with self and friend, a gentle thread that has no end.
Practice daily, soft and true, peace will rise and walk with you.

The Wheel of Life

Picture your life as a circle, a pie, each slice is a part that helps you get by. Career and finances, the work that you do, health, recreation, and friendships too.

Romance and family, the people you love, growth and learning, the stars up above. Each piece of the wheel plays its own role, together they balance the life of the whole.

If one slice is tiny while others are wide, the wheel turns uneven, it wobbles, won't glide. But when all are steady, in harmony spun, life rolls much smoother, more balanced, more fun.

So, check on your wheel, let each slice be bright, for balance brings peace and your journey feels right.

WHEEL OF LIFE

The Gut-Brain Axis

Deep in your belly, a story is told, of nerves and of microbes, both timid and bold. A two-way connection, a whisper, a song, between gut and the brain, where signals belong.

The vagus nerve travels, a wandering guide, carrying messages back and forth, side to side. It links how you're thinking with what you digest, a harmony hidden within your own chest.

The gut makes transmitters, serotonin, the key, shaping your mood and your mind's melody. Dopamine too joins the chemical stream, fuelling your focus, your joy, and your dream.

Trillions of microbes, a bustling crowd, sending out signals both subtle and loud. They fashion small messengers, shaping your mind, proof that the body and brain are entwined.

The enteric system, the second brain near, guides how digestion runs smooth and clear. Independent yet speaking, it knows what to do, a partner in health, always talking to you.

So, stress may cause butterflies, nausea, or pain, while diet can brighten or darken the brain. This axis reminds us, through science and art, the gut and the mind are never apart.

Tapping the Path to Calm

Beneath the arm, the spleen does sigh, worry and failure come drifting by. Under the eye where the stomach lies, anxious thoughts and low esteem rise.

On the nail of the index near the thumb, the large intestine's stories come. Confusion, grief, rejection's song, a sadness that's been held too long.

The thumb itself, the lung's own place, carries shame upon its face. Defensive walls, the tears held tight, bullying shadows dim the light.

Upon the chest where the liver rests, bitterness, anger, guilt confess. By the temple, gallbladder we see, frustration, panic, and discouraged plea.

The back of the hand, the triple flame, pericardium's middle finger bears the same. Shock, humiliation, jealousy's sting, unworthy feelings the tapping can bring.

Collarbone low, where kidneys stay, fear and hatred find their way. The brow's beginning, bladder near, paranoia, blame, depression appear.

The little finger outside we find, small intestine speaks the mind. Alone, betrayed, or left behind, sad and empty, lost in time.

Inside the nail, the heart does weep, jealous unloved, in shadows deep. Yet tapping through each tender part, brings back the strength within the heart.

THE SHAPES THE BODY SPEAKS

BOUNDARIES

DRAMA

CIRCLES

SPIRALS

FLOWERS

PATTERNS

THE SECRET SYMBOLS YOUR BODY SPEAKS.

Your body talks in shapes and signs, in quiet ways, between the lines.
A square says "boundaries, keep it tight," It's solid, stable, grounded right.

Triangles balance, sharp and clean, a mix of calm and energy seen. They point to growth, to rising high, a symbol of the mind and sky.

A circle flows, no start or end, It loops around like time, my friend.
Wholeness, unity, going strong like planets spinning all along.

The spiral's wild, it moves, it grows, like galaxies or how life flows. It mirrors change, a shifting track a winding path that pulls you back.

And flowers? Patterns deep and bright, they map the way life holds the light.
Each petal, perfect, placed with care a sign we're all connected there.

Each shape has vibes it's not just art, they hit you right inside the heart.
They hum in tune with how we live, with energy they freely give.

From ocean shells to bodies' curves, to every line the planet serves. These shapes are keys to something more, a code that opens inner doors.

So, use them when you paint or pray, or just to guide you through the day.
They help align; they help you see there's quiet truth in geometry.

Loving a Bit of Drama

Do you ever feel despite what you do, that drama keeps finding it's way back to you? You dodge, you weave, you try to be wise, but chaos keeps knocking, wearing disguise.

You might not notice, at first, when it starts, a sigh, a complaint, some wounded hearts. But soon you're cast in a three-part show, a triangle dance you didn't know.

There's the victim, feeling helpless and small, "No one understands me at all." Then comes the rescuer, cape in hand, fixing what they don't quite understand.

The persecutor points and blames, fuelling guilt and fanning flames. Three roles we play, in loops so tight, each one certain they're in the right.

These roles aren't who you truly are, they're echoes of an older scar. Maybe, you learned, back in the day, love came with games you had to play.

Attachment strained, or care withheld, emotions you never fully spelled. Or perhaps you met a charm so grand, narcissism dressed in a helping hand.

It's easy to slip into scripts so old, where drama feels familiar, bold. But here's the truth, you have a voice, to stand your ground, to make a choice. Compassion helps. So does space. Not every problem needs to be chased.

You're not a saviour, you're not to blame. You don't have to play the game. You can respond instead of react, with conscious care, and inner tact. So next time drama comes to dine, you don't have to pour the wine.

If this triangle feels like home, know you're not walking it alone. Let others play if they must, but you can choose to build self-trust.

Beyond the Letters

They give us letters, one by one ADHD, and then some. ADD, BPD too, as if those words define what's true.

But are we just the names they say, the labels stuck to us each day? Do they decide what we can be, or hold the key to "you" or "me"?

No, not if we refuse to bind our worth to what they've underlined. For deep inside, there burns a flame, untouched by letters, titles, shame.

Our dreams don't need a doctor's file to run their course or stretch a mile. Desires that rise from deep within aren't lessened by the state we're in.

Look inward, not to hide or flee, but find your truth and set it free. You're more than what the world may see, a soul beyond a summary.

So don't let labels draw the line, you're built to grow, to rise, to shine. Not just a name or brain design, but something greater. Something divine.

Only Love Can Light the Way

In streets where silence echoes pain, where hearts are bruised by hate's refrain. A voice still rises through the years, a call that soothes the heart that hears.

He said that hate can't banish hate, only love can shift the weight. Yet still the world ignores the call, as fear and cruelty touch us all.

But kindness is a quiet flame, It does not shout, it does not blame. It heals the wounds we cannot see; it breaks the chains and sets us free.

If one kind act can shift the tide, if one brave soul stands dignified. Then hope returns, not loud, but true, a single light the dark breaks through.

We crave a world where peace is born, where justice stands, not bruised or torn. Where colour, creed, and love unite to turn the wrong and pain to right.

Let's choose the harder path each day, to lift, not crush, to build, not fray. For anger fades and hate decays, but only love can light the way.

Life's Journey

The road of life is never straight, with doors that close and hands of fate. Yet every turn, each step we take, can shape the dreams we long to make.

Through trials faced, our hearts grow strong, the darkest night won't last for long. Beyond the storm, the skies turn clear, and brighter paths will soon appear.

Each dream we hold, each hope we find, becomes a compass for the mind. A steady flame, a guiding star, to show us who we truly are.

The journey shines with lessons deep, with love to give and joy to keep. Though the road may twist and bend, its beauty lasts until the end.

So, walk with courage, trust the skies, for every season, new wings will rise. Life's greatest gift is not the goal but growing into your own soul.

REIKI

THE GIFT OF REIKI

Reiki is gentle, a soft flowing stream, a current of light, a deep healing dream. It soothes away tension, releases the pain, and helps your own wholeness awaken again.

It's not someone fixing, or magic on show, but stirring the power you already know. A touch that reminds you of wisdom inside, where body and spirit in balance reside.

It's calm and relaxing, a moment of peace, a place where the chatter of worry can cease. It lightens the heart and it quiets the mind, restoring alignment with all that's divine.

It's never religion, control, or a game, no dogma, no pressure, no guilt and no shame. It partners with doctors, with therapy too, enhancing the healing that's waiting in you.

Not "woo-woo" or trickery, yet magic may start, when harmony ripples through body and heart. For Reiki's a whisper, a yes soft and true, to love, to your energy, to the real you!

THE VOICE WITHIN

A whisper tells me I'm not enough, that every climb will be too tough. It questions dreams, it plants the fear, that failure waits if I draw near.

It hides behind each choice I make, it shakes my hands, it makes me break, it steals the colours from my skies, and clouds the truth with tangled lies.

Yet somewhere deep, a softer tone, reminds me I'm not all alone, that doubt is just a passing guest, not proof I'll falter in the test.

For every stumble shapes the ground, where surer footsteps can be found. And though self-doubt may dim the flame, I'll rise, and try, and try again.

After the Blast

The night was meant for song and cheer, yet shadows broke the music clear, a single act, so cruel, so fast, forever marked us with the blast.

The echoes linger, sharp and deep, in waking thoughts, in haunted sleep. For loss was heavy, hearts undone, yet still we rise to greet the sun.

Though grief may whisper, fear may stay, each step is courage, day by day, for healing's path is slow, not straight, but love walks with us, strong as fate.

No pain is lesser, none too small, each wounded heart deserves recall, and in this web of care we find, a gentler place for soul and mind.

So let the silence hold the name, of every life, of every flame, and may compassion's steady light, guide broken spirits through the night.

The Mask of Doubt

A voice inside those whispers low, you don't belong, they'll surely know, though skills are real, the mind's unkind, imposter thoughts can cloud the mind.

Perfection's weight, a heavy chain, no effort feels quite worth the gain. The bar is set beyond the sky, and missing it brings shame, not why.

A childhood filled with praise or blame, with pressure tied to worth and name, can sow the seeds of deep unease, where winning means you might appease.

In halls of work or schools so bright, new places spark the hidden fight. Where eyes compare and standards gleam, the fraud within begins to scheme.

To feel apart, the lone one there, by race or gender, age or care. Can make the self retreat, conceal, and question if one's place is real.

Society, with rigid views, can cast its doubt, distort, confuse. Its stereotypes, unfair, untrue, can weigh on hearts and shape the view.

Yet know this truth, you are not flawed, these doubts are built by life's façade. It isn't weakness, but the blend, of self and world, you must transcend.

So, when you feel that you're a sham, remember who you truly am. Your worth is here, it's not pretend, the voice of doubt is not the end.

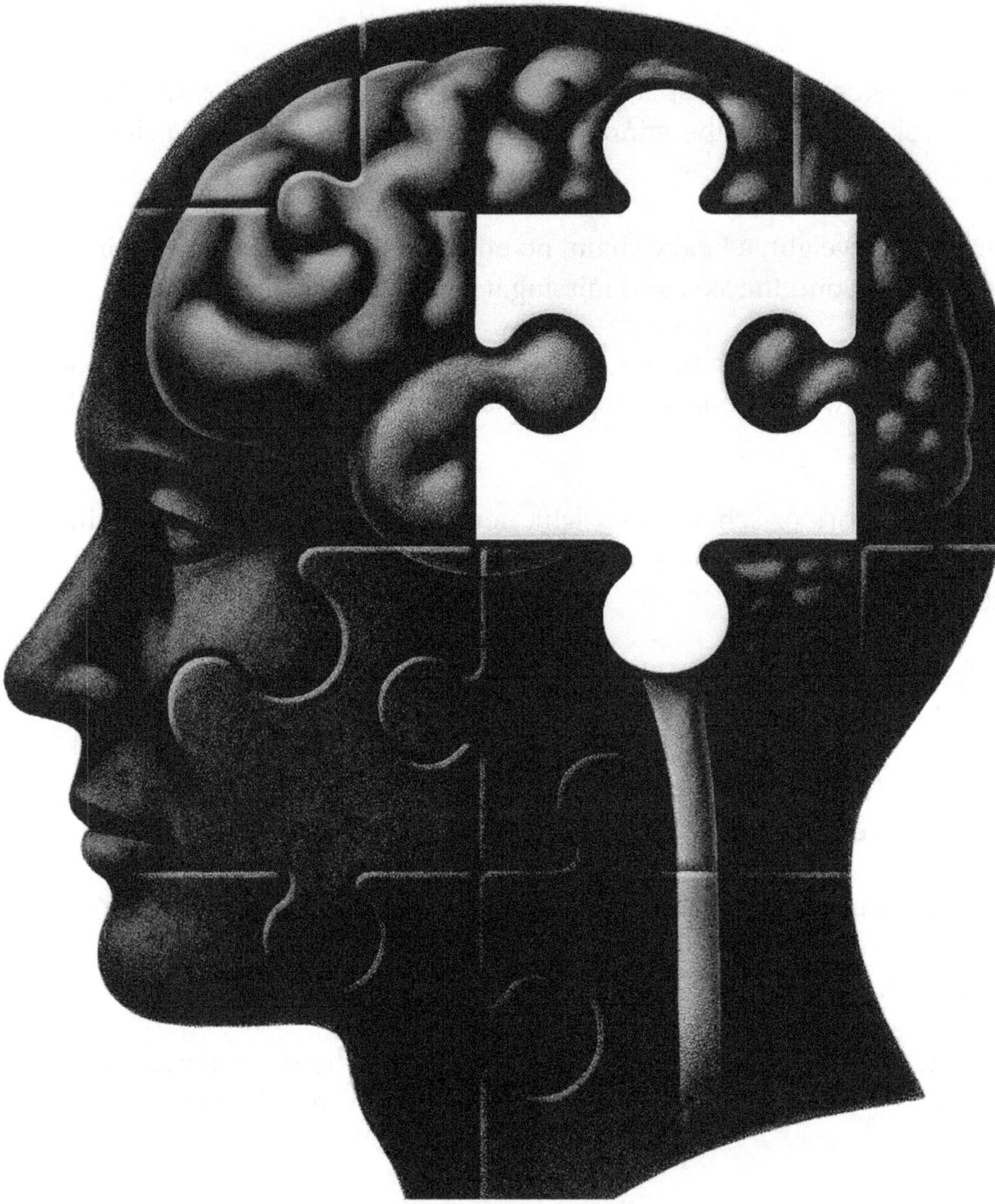

Thinking About Thinking

I'm thinking about thinking, a mirror in the mind, a lantern in the labyrinth, a way to seek and find.

It whispers how I'm learning, reveals my hidden flaws, it pauses when I'm struggling, and questions why I pause.

It charts my strengths and weaknesses, it measures how I grow, it tells me when to linger, and when to let things go.

It guides my problem-solving, a compass in the storm, it bends and shifts my strategies to help new pathways form.

It's more than thought, it's watching thought, a second, deeper sight, metacognition, self-aware, a candle in the night.

With practice it grows sharper, this self-reflective art, to set my goals, refine my ways, and train both mind and heart.

So, thinking about thinking is more than just a game, it's knowing how I come to know, and never thinking quite the same.

Glow Through Change

Begin with the whole, not the part, sketch the outline, make a start. Change feels heavy, tangled, wide but maps bring light to what's inside.

Keep it simple, five steps, maybe ten don't rush the "how," just name the "when." In twenty minutes, draw the frame, you'll see the path won't look the same.

Notice the forks, the stops, the bends, where fear begins, and hope extends. A flowchart isn't carved in stone, it shows you're moving, not alone.

Break it down, one task, one day, a small step forward clears the way. Patterns emerge where once was blur, You'll find the glow you thought unsure.

End with insight, calm, and grace, your journey mapped becomes a space. Where healing grows, where courage starts, a living chart of human hearts.

The Box Breath

When life feels heavy, storm clouds near, a simple tool can make it clear. No pills, no fuss, no grand design, breath and rhythm, slow, in time.

Inhale through the nose, count four, hold it gently, nothing more. Exhale softly, four beats long, hold again, you're growing strong.

This pattern wakes a hidden thread, the vagus nerve, from toes to head. It whispers calm, it soothes the chest, it guides the body back to rest.

Cortisol begins to fall, your heartbeat steadies, strong, yet small. The amygdala softens fear's loud cries, the prefrontal clears and sharpens the skies.

A minute or two will ease the weight, five brings calm to re-regulate. Ten each day builds strength anew, resilience rising, tried and true.

Before a meeting, when sleep won't stay or stress would steal your breath away. Box breathing steadies, clears the night, a quiet lantern, soft with light.

So, when the world feels sharp, ask why, then pause, breathe deep, and let it fly. For even ninety seconds spent, can shift the soul to calm content.

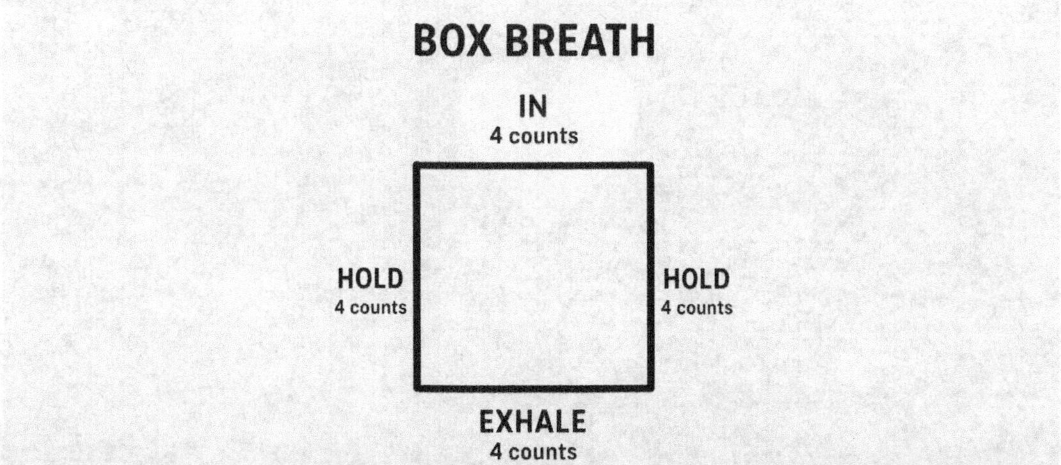

Reach for Your Stars

The world can be loud, with people who say, do things like me, and live my way. But deep in your heart is a compass, a flame, it whispers your truth, it calls out your name.

Don't measure your worth by the mask's others wear, their paths are not yours, their burdens not fair. Your values, your dreams are the map in your hand, to guide you with courage, like stars in the sand.

When storms cloud your sky and you feel torn apart, remember the strength that lives in your heart. You're more than the fears that try to confine, your purpose is waiting, uniquely divine.

So, reach for the stars that belong just to you, a life built on meaning, on love that is true. Stand tall in your being, let your spirit take flight, your journey is precious your own guiding light.

The Silent Feast

We eat to feel comfort, or starve to feel strong, a battle with food we've been fighting too long. The plate becomes prison, the fork holds the key, a story of self, shaped by pain we can't see.

Anorexia whispers, be thinner, be less, a hunger for safety, disguised as success. But beneath the restriction, a child aches inside, longing for love, yet compelled to hide.

Bulimia shouts, let it out, take control, yet purging just deepens the ache of the soul. It's guilt, self-rejection, a cycle of shame, throwing up sorrow, but feeling the same.

Orthorexia prays, eat pure, never stray, but health turns to prison in a different way. Anxiety isolates, joy fades to grey, when fear of "unhealthy" steals life's play.

ARFID retreats, its textures, its taste, a world that feels frightening, too much to face. For some neurodivergent, it's part of their mind, feeling too different, no safety to find.

Polyphagia hungers, insatiable need, no signal of fullness, no rest from the feed. Genes, or the meds, or a brain out of tune, it's chasing a fullness that never comes soon.

Pica still whispers, eat what should not, the body seeks something the spirit forgot. Strange cravings for safety, for grounding, for more, searching for meaning in what we explore.

And behind it all, fear hides in disguise, Emetophobia terror lives deep in the eyes. Avoidance, restriction, obsession, control the dread of being sick grips body and soul.

Yet all of these voices, though twisted by pain, are echoes of longing, repeating the same. A wish to feel safe, to belong, to be free, a cry for connection, for love, just to be.

Addiction

I wasn't the one who broke the rules, but somehow still, I bore the tools, to fix, to patch, to clean the mess, to carry burdens I won't confess.

The house went still, then shook with cries, while you were gone, I dried her eyes. I cleaned the mess; I played it cool and shoved my fury back to school.

They called you sick, they said disease, while I stayed quiet, begging peace. I watched you fall; I felt the blow and still you chose that undertow.

You stole the stage with every fall, the fights, the lies, the frantic calls. While I grew up too fast, too soon, you chased your high beneath the moon.

Was I the lucky one? I guess. I passed my tests. I caused no stress. But love felt rationed, thinly spread, while you were sick, I starved instead.

I hated you. Then hated me, for wishing you'd just let us be. I wore the mask of "doing fine," while wishing I could draw the line.

I've read the books, I've tried to learn, that pain like yours can twist and turn. That choice runs out where need begins, that shame won't help you shed your sins.

No lesson learned can make it new, the time I lost, the love gone too. I cared for you, but here I stand, no fuel remains within my hand.

So, here's my truth, I'm finding me. Not just your shadow, not debris. I'll cheer you on, but from my shore, a sibling's love, but nothing more.

The Gentle Art of Letting Go

I carry wounds I cannot see, some made by others, some by me. A heavy heart, a silent ache, from all the choices we both make.

But now I pause, I breathe, I feel and give myself the time to heal. No need to hide, no need to flee, my hurt deserves to speak through me.

I name the pain, I let it stay, then gently guide it on its way. For holding on does not make right it only dims my inner light.

To those who caused a tear or scar, I see how broken people are. Not all with harm in heart begin, sometimes we lash from pain within.

I won't excuse; I won't defend but choose the path that helps me mend. The rage, the weight, the urge to fight, I trade them for my peace tonight.

And when it's me who played a part, I turn with kindness to my heart. I own the wrong, I make things new and grow through what I thought I knew.

Forgiveness is a door I choose, for healing more than what I lose. Each time I stumble, still I rise, with clearer heart and kinder eyes.

So here I stand, both hurt and whole, with open hands and mended soul. I won't forget, but I will grow, that is the art of letting go.

fear
failure
doubt
trust
love
growth

Hope From the Hopelessness

When shadows stretch across your mind, and every light feels hard to find, when silence roars and drowns your plea, please know, it's not the end you'll see.

You're not alone, though pain runs deep, though heavy thoughts disturb your sleep. This aching heart, this tightening chest, are messengers, not foes to wrest.

So breathe. Just once. Then breathe again. You don't have to escape the pain. Let sorrow speak, let anger cry, emotions pass they do not lie. Don't chase the sun or curse the rain, or try to run from inner strain.

Sit with it all, don't shrink or flee, acceptance is the first soft key. It's not defeat to feel this way, you're human, made of night and day. But in the stillness, cracks appear, and through them, light will draw more near.

Small acts of care just one, then two can shift the world inside of you. A call, a walk, a whispered prayer, a moment just to breathe the air. Gratitude's a quiet spark, that flickers gently in the dark.

Name one good thing then maybe more, a step, a laugh, an open door. Your thoughts may say, "This is the end." but thoughts aren't always truth, my friend.

You can reframe, release, revise see through the fear with wiser eyes. And if you fall, then fall with grace, not as a shame, but sacred place.

The soil of struggle grows the soul and broken parts can make you whole. So if you're lost, just start with this, not every wound comes without bliss. Hope isn't loud, or always near but it will come. Just stay right here.

LOOK
INSIDE
N
W
E
S
START
END

A Map Back to Me

Are you storing emotions deep inside? where do they linger, where do they hide? Take a moment, pause, and feel, your body speaks what you don't reveal.

Neck so stiff, can't turn with ease, are you choking back the words that tease? A bottled voice, a silent cry, a life not lived, a stifled why?

Jaw that clenches through the night, holding anger, hiding fight. The words you swallowed, left unsaid, now live where tension tucks in bed.

Shoulders heavy, burdened low, carrying more than you let show. Responsibility you never chose, feel it there, beneath your clothes.

Chest is tight with unshed tears, a haven for your deepest fears. Heartbreak's weight and grief so vast, linger here until they're passed.

Hands that shake or tightly close, grasping hard to gain control. Overwhelmed and needing grace, afraid to trust the flow you face.

Stomach churns, knots inside, digesting truths that you must hide. A punch of words, a twist of pain, the gut remembers all you feign.

Lower back begins to ache, support you lack or risks you take. Worries around your home or pay, your spine absorbs them every day.

Hips hold grief you never knew, emotions buried, overdue. Stretch and weep, release the ache, let your body start to break.

Knees that fear the path ahead, long to move but freeze instead. Uncertain steps, a need to know, keeps you stuck when life says "go."

So, scan your form, from head to toe, and listen to what it wants to show. Your body holds what mind forgets, in tension, pain, and deep regrets.

But also, there beneath the strife, is your roadmap back to life. Release, express, begin to feel, for that's the way the body heals.

The Id, Ego & Superego

Inside my head, a trio lives, each one takes, and each one gives. They shape the way I think and feel a team of three behind the wheel.

The Id a hungry kid, wants what it wants, just like it did. "More cake!" it shouts, "I want it now!" no rules, no wait, no why or how. It doesn't care what's right or wrong, it's all desire, loud and strong. Sleep, fun, food, the craving crew, all impulse, passion breaking through.

The Ego's job is to stay calm and cool, it listens well and plays by rule. I could change here, but eyes might peek, I'll find a place that's safe and sleek.

At last, the Superego speaks, with wisdom, morals, rules it keeps. It's like a voice that knows what's right, a guide that shines a conscience light.

Like when I race, and no one sees, a shortcut path between the trees, I could cheat once to win the gold, but guilt steps in, and breaks that hold.

So, in my mind, three parts combine, the wild, the wise, the drawn-in line. Id wants now, and Ego thinks, Superego checks the links.

And that's the trio me, but three, all pulling strings inside of me. Each has a role, a voice, a say and who I am is how they play.

The Core of Us

We are seekers, made to roam, chasing stars yet pulled by home. A spark that says, "Go start, begin", to leap, to grow, to dive within.

We long to laugh, to cry, be seen, to sit where open hearts have been. To feel the warmth of love held tight, connection is our guiding light.

We crave a calm, a steady base, but fear can flare when cracks replace. We fight, we freeze, or flee the night, then anger burns to make things right.

From rage, a sense of justice grows, it names the hurt, it calls it close. We need the space to breathe, to play, to shake the weight of every day.

Autonomy, our sacred thread, not led by force, but choice instead. A compass carved in self and skin, to find the truth that lives within.

In stillness, where our hearts unfold, we meet ourselves, both shy and bold. We touch another, soul to soul, where love, not lust, can make us whole.

And when we lose what once was near, grief howls loud, then whispers clear. Yet healing waits where love once grew, and strength builds slowly, deep and true.

We rise to feel, not just to win, to breathe, to move, to dance within. We're more than minds that plan and scheme, we're living vessels, dream by dream.

So, ask, "What makes us real, and true?" It's how we love, connect, and choose. A quiet fire beneath the skin, the core of us, the place within.

Blades Don't Heal

You carry it deep in your pocket, a fear you don't show on your face. A blade becomes your silence, your shield in a violent place.

They say it's just for protection, a "just in case" kind of thing. But one quick choice in panic now it's pain that your hands bring.

One moment, gone in a heartbeat, a life cut short by pride, and now you're stuck with nightmares, you can't outrun or hide.

The streets weren't meant to raise you, they're cold, and hard, and loud. They cheer you on in madness but vanish when you're down.

You say, "They don't know how it feels, the pressure, the rage, the fear", but carrying knives is a silence that only draws pain near.

Someone Else's Dream

Do you ever wake and feel the ache, a hollow place you can't explain. Like life's a play you didn't write yet still perform each endless night.

We chase the maps that others drew, mistake their wants for something true. But in the mirror, what we find is not our soul just borrowed time.

We dressed in dreams that weren't our size, wore smiles to meet approving eyes, but underneath the silent screams of lives un-lived and strangled dreams.

They told us what success should be, what love should look like how to see. But no one asked what makes us whole, or what would satisfy the soul.

We scroll through lives that shine so bright, greenest grass in filtered light. While ours feels dim, we chase and chase a quiet, slow, un-winnable race.

But what if we could just let go of all the things we've come to know. Strip off the weight of their desire, and light our own, unrented fire.

Perhaps the path was always ours, not paved in gold, but lined with stars. And once we let the noise drift by, our own true voice will rise and fly.

Grounding

Be well-rounded, whole, and real, we must return to what we feel. Not just the thoughts that cloud the skies, but the Earth below, where stillness lies. How does it work? you ask with a sigh, it's not in the head, but the soil where we try. Alignment begins with a single breath, a pause, a space, a step from stress.

When the mind runs fast and the heart feels sore, the Earth can open a quieter door. Electric whispers from root to skin, the ground invites us to sink back in. A barefoot step on morning dew reminds the soul what's good and true.

The grass beneath, the breeze above, reveals a deeper kind of love. In anxious waves or heavy days, nature steadies, soothes, and stays.

In silence, in soil, in softening pace, we find again our native grace. So, stand in mud, or walk on stone, you're not adrift, you're not alone. To ground is to come back home inside, where healing and hope gently reside.

Breathe Into Movement

Move slow, stretch wide, let your body wake inside. In whispers soft, the muscles sigh, a dance of strength and grace nearby. Balance blooms like quiet light, rooted deep in calm twilight.

Tension drips like morning dew, stress dissolves as breath flows through. Posture rises, pain retreats, heart and lungs in steady beats. More than motion, more than pose, a journey inward, where self grows.

A tender space where silence sings, and healing folds its gentle wings. Here, in breath and body's flow, the seeds of peace begin to grow. A sacred meeting, soft and slow, the art of coming home, you know.

It's Not You, It's Safety!

You don't need hustle, you don't need grind, you're not falling behind, you just need a safe mind.

Your brain's on alert, not lazy or stuck. It is scanning for danger, not chasing luck.

When things feel heavy, you shut down fast, that's not failure, that's built to last.

It's not a lack of fire or fight, your system's just protecting right.

But when you see what dims your flame and stop the self blame game.
That's when it shifts, that's when you flow, that's when you rise and start to grow.

In the Wake of Loss

Are you alone, adrift, and grieving, caught in the quiet ache of leaving? Loss is absence, deep and wide, not just death, but shifts inside. It may be love, a role, a face, health or hope that's lost its place.

Grief responds in waves and storm, in every feeling, shape, and form. Sadness, anger, numbness, pain, guilt confusion all remain. Aching hearts, sleep torn away, joy feels distant, far from day.

Let your feelings come and go, there is no need to rush the flow. Speak with those who understand, reach for love, extend your hand. Find small rhythms, tend your care, honour memories, keep them there.

Though life has changed, new paths appear and healing whispers, soft but clear. Grief is love that has no end, but with time, the soul can mend.

The Art of Listening

Some only pause, just waiting to talk, their minds on reply, not on your walk. They're silent, yes but not really there, just framing words to toss in the air.

Some catch your voice in bits and threads but wander off inside their heads. They nod along, then drift away half in the room, half gone astray.

But others stop and truly hear, your words ring sharp, your meaning clear. They're not just waiting for their turn, they're here to listen, learn, discern.

And deeper still, some feel your tone, the hurt you carry, not yet shown. They sense the storm behind your eyes; they hear your truth beneath disguise.

The rarest ones hear what's unsaid, the weight that hangs, the thoughts you've shed. They're fully present, heart and mind, the kind of soul that's hard to find.

So, listen close, both heart and ear, through every doubt and fleeting fear. For when we choose to truly hear, we make our voices strong and clear.

Whispers Within.

Inside the hush beneath the skin, where quiet truths and thoughts begin. A hidden sense begins to speak, not loud, but steady, strong, and meek.

It tells of hunger, thirst, and pain, of beating hearts and thoughts that strain. A whisper rising through the nerves, in patterns only feeling serves.

From muscle, organ, skin, and bone, these signals travel all alone. Until they reach the mind's great sea a storm of thought and memory.

The brain receives, it weaves, it blends, it listens close, it comprehends. And from this thread of silent cues, it paints the body's inner news.

A thirst becomes a need to drink; a fluttered pulse invites us: think. A tense jaw, clenched with quiet fight, reveals the edge of inner fright.

So interoception takes its place, a mirror of the inner space. It links the body, mind, and soul, and makes the unseen senses whole.

In every heartbeat, breath, or chill, the body speaks, if we sit still. To feel within is to be wise to see the world through inward eyes.

Manifesting

Manifesting isn't daydreams, or hoping life is what it seems. It's matching thought with how you move, a quiet focus, inner groove.

Start by knowing what you seek, get specific, not mystique. Picture it like it's already real, feel the joy, the drive, the zeal.

Speak it out, affirm it true, "I'm becoming what I do." Train your mind to see the way, even when it's not today.

Keep your vibe on something higher, as gratitude becomes your fire.
Positivity's not just fluff, it helps you rise when life gets tough.

But here's the part some people skip: You've got to take that daily trip.
Inspired steps, small but clear, show the world that you're sincere.

Trust the timing, let it flow, let your effort help it grow. When signs appear, don't second-guess, that's the process saying "yes."

It's mindset, movement, energy becoming who you're meant to be. No spells, no tricks, no fairy dust, just showing up and building trust.

The Eyes Remember

They say the eyes reflect the soul, a place where stories take their toll. They shine with joy, or hide the fear, and hold the things we won't go near.

A glance can smile, a look can lie, and still, the pain won't pass us by. We cover wounds with calm and grace but hurt still lingers in the face.

We hide it deep and wear a smile, but healing walks a different mile.
That's where eye movements start, a gentle path back through the heart.
The eyes shift left, then to the right, like stepping through the edge of night.

Retracing roads we've tried to flee, but now with strength to set us free.
A rhythm slow, a steady guide, to meet the pain, we've pushed aside. But this time, we are not the same, we speak the fear, we name the name.

The grip it had begins to fade, the memory starts to lose its blade. It doesn't mean we just forget, but now, we carry less regret. The weight we held, tight and long, can leave us so we feel strong. The eyes once trapped by things we saw now open wide with softer awe. They still remember but with grace to let the soul find a safer space.

Still Me!

I've got a habit no, not that kind, it's more in the corners of my mind. Not bottles or smoke, no dice or deals, it's chasing approval on hamster wheels. I scroll and compare, I strive and pretend, to keep up with peers I don't even call friends. I laugh at the parties, I nod and I grin, but I'm wondering quietly, "Where do I fit in?"

My worth's on a diet it's running quite low, fed by the likes and the status quo. Somehow, I'm hooked on the need to belong, even when something feels terribly wrong.

I get stuck in loops, rewinding old doubt, looking for reasons to count myself out. But deep down a whisper begins to unfold, I'm enough as I am, not bought, not sold.

So maybe I'm 'addicted' to proving I'm fine, but healing, I hear, takes a little time. And hey, I'm still learning, still tripping, still me, just trying to set my own spirit free.

So, here's to the journey, both rocky and bright, to laughter, to growth, to sleeping at night. To choosing self-love when the critics appear, and quietly telling them, thanks, I'm good here.

THE WORRY THAT WAKES US!

Anxiety whispers in the quiet night, a shadow stirred by future's light. A racing heart, a restless mind, searching for threats it cannot find. It's natural, a part of you, a signal flashing danger through.

Like standing poised before a test, your body braces, won't let rest. It starts with thoughts that softly grow, a sense of dread you barely know.

Worry tightens, takes its seat, in trembling hands and heavy feet. Muscles clench, your breathing's tight, sleep slips off into the night. A stomach turns, your head may ache, all from fears that start to wake.

It's helpful sometimes, keeps us safe, a call to slow down, guard our pace. But when it stays, both day and night, it dims your joy and steals your light.

When it begins to take control, to blur your mind and weigh your soul. When it makes it hard to live or cope, that's when you know you must find hope.

You're not alone in how this feels, there's strength in naming what it steals. With time and care, support and grace, you'll learn to meet it face to face. So, if your thoughts run far and wide, know, that you can turn the tide. Anxiety though loud and real is something you can learn to heal.

The Frequency Within

They say all things are made of light, that matter hums in hidden flight. Einstein whispered through the veil: "Energy and mass prevail."$E = mc^2$, a truth so bright the universe, in waves of light.

Your body, too, is not just bone, but pulses tuned to tones unknown. A field of charge, a song, a spark, that dances in the silent dark. Each cell responds to sound and wave, to love, to thought, to how you behave.

In 2025, we start to see a healing truth in frequency. No longer myth, no longer guess, we chart the sound of happiness. From brainwaves calm to heartbeats strong, the proof was pulsing all along.

Reiki flows with gentle hands, no pill, no cut, no harsh demands. Just energy from source to skin, a sacred warmth that heals within. The body knows what it must do when touched by something pure and true.

And EFT, with tapping light, can shift the soul from fear to flight. A rhythm touched on meridian streams can silence old and looping dreams.
The past unwinds, the pain releases, the heart, once cracked, finds newer pieces.

This isn't faith without the facts, nor science lost to ancient acts. It's fusion proof and intuition, a future framed by clearer vision.

Where healing meets the inner quest, and energy becomes our best. We grow not just in body, mind, but in the soul we long to find.

Through frequency, we start to see that healing is remembering "me." Not just the name, or face, or role, but the pulsing truth beneath it all.

So, tune your breath, align your tone, you're made of stars not flesh alone.
In every beat, a sacred code a quantum path, a healing road.
The medicine of future days will echo light in subtle ways.
And when they ask what made you whole, you'll smile and say "I healed my soul."

The Climb

At the base of the pyramid, hunger and thirst, we seek out the simplest needs to quench first. Warmth in the cold, and rest when we're tired, the breath of survival is deeply required.

Next comes a longing for safety and peace, a haven where danger and chaos can cease. We build up our walls, and we lock every door, but fear still can rattle the bones at our core.

Then rises the ache just to feel, we're not lone, to matter to someone, to be truly known. We cling to connection, to love that won't fade, but too many heartbreaks can dull what we crave.

Esteem is the fourth oh, the battle for pride, to stand on our merits, with nothing to hide. But chasing approval in an unsteady race can fracture our minds and erode our own grace.

At the peak stands the call to become who we are, to stretch past the clouds and reach for the stars. But how can we grow, become something grand, if life's lower layers are slipping like sand.

Emotional overload comes like a flood, when the pyramid crumbles and crashes in mud. We try to ascend, but we're not on firm ground, and feelings explode when we're safety unbound.

To thrive, we must tend to each level with care, not rush to the top, just to say we are there. For when we ignore what the heart truly pleads, we drown in the weight of our unmet needs.

If I were a Puzzle

If I were a puzzle, scattered and wide, forever searching for pieces outside. Competing with forces I couldn't quite name, longing for wholeness, yet feeling the same.

Craving a place where I might belong, a sense of worth I've chased all along. But the truth is whispered from the start, the answers lie deep in the chambers of heart.

We look outside, spinning round and round, missing the stillness where truth is found. We chase what's missing in outer space, forgetting the pieces we already face.

No borrowed pieces can make us whole, only silence can speak to a restless soul. For puzzles with gaps weigh heavy and dense, cluttering our spirit, defying all sense.

A puzzle with no edges, no clear frame, leaves us breathless, caught in blame. Our hearts forget their rhythm and beat, lost in a cycle, incomplete yet when we turn inward, soft and still, we start to remember, we start to feel, then heal.

The programme fades, the noise grows thin, we hear the voice that lives within. Yes, we may live with pieces misplaced, with wounds unspoken, and fears we face.

The what ifs, the if only's tear us apart, yet what if our story reflects who we are? What if the cracks, the missing design, is part of the picture by some grand design?

A mirror not broken, but waiting to show, the beauty within we've yet to know. Each jagged edge, each piece we've denied, was never meant to be cast aside.

So, if I were a puzzle, unfinished, unsure, I'd stop seeking pieces behind every door. I'd look in the silence, the stillness, the space, and there, I'd begin to find my place.

You Can't Have Your Cake and Eat It Too!

We wired the brain to chase delight, a burst of joy, a screen-lit night. Dopamine whispers, soft and sweet, a fleeting taste, then quick retreat.

We want the calm, the quiet mind, but scroll through noise we hope to find. A soothing balm, a thought subdued, while feeding habits that intrude.

You want the peace, the still, the true, but skip the work it takes to do. The therapy, the sleepless tears, the long unlearning of the years.

You want to run, avoid the ache, yet wish your heart would never break. To numb the pain yet feel alive the brain won't let both states survive.

You want your cake the sugar high, the perfect mask, the perfect lie. But eat it too? The cost is steep the mind will take what you can't keep.

So, here's the truth, both kind and stark, the brain remembers every mark. To heal, you walk through fire and rain, the long, slow rewiring of the brain.

You can have joy, and peace, and grace, but not without first facing place, the shadowed parts, the hidden view, you can't have cake and eat it too.

Staying on Track

In classrooms and in living rooms, some tempers flare, some chaos blooms. A slammed down door, a lie, a shout, the kind of storm we talk about.

But kids aren't bad, they've lost their way, their hearts are learning day by day. Respect's not born, it's gently taught, through love and time, and patient thought.

When words come sharp, don't fight with fire, don't meet their rage with your own ire. Sit down, breathe deep, and start to share, I feel hurt, not you don't care."

Listen close to what they mean, even anger hides unseen. A lonely heart, a worried mind, with open ears, the truth you'll find.

Talk it out, not lecture loud, stay calm, stay kind, but firm and proud. Build trust that grows through every talk, a bridge of care where both can walk.

Teens will push, it's what they do, they're finding selves, they're learning too. So guide them firm, but give them space, and meet defiance with steady grace.

Keep watch for friends, for screens, for shows, the things that shape the way one grows. Teach them what's real, what's just pretend, and show that peace is strength, my friend.

Set clear rules and stay consistent, gentle hearts but firm, persistent. Boundaries made with love, not fear, help kids feel safe, respected, clear.

When anger hits, help find a way, to pause, to breathe, to cool the fray. Say let's talk once calm returns, we'll find the lesson, not just burns.

Teach empathy, how would *you* feel if harsh words cut, or truths weren't real. That simple step, when hearts connect, can turn defiance into respect.

Don't call them rude, or lost, or bad, those words can stick and make hearts sad. Say that choice was wrong, then guide again, mistakes are steps, they help us mend.

So, parents, carers take your part, lead not with power, but with heart. The road to growth is never flat but love and patience carry that.

And kids, remember every day, respect and kindness light your way. The choices now, both big and small, can *build* a life that stands tall.

The Living Antenna, The Mind: The Meaning Maker and the Universe

The Living Antenna

Your body's more than skin and bone,
it senses more than what's been shown.
A living system tuned and clear,
responding to what moves it near.

The vagus nerve, the fascia's thread,
feel sound and light, what's done and said.
Each field, each tone, each subtle cue,
the body reads and echoes too.

Our memories live in flesh and frame,
In breath, in pulse, in muscle's name.
A trauma stored, a rhythm learned,
can shape the way the heart is turned.

Our bodies match the world's design
We move in step with space and time.
The beat of drums, the rise of sun,
Remind the body all is one.

Your body, through its pulse and tone,
Translates the universe your own.

The Mind: The Meaning Maker

Between the cells and what we feel,
the mind gives shape, it turns the wheel.
Perception shifts what's seen and true
Belief creates what bodies do.
Neural paths will bend and grow,
where focus goes, the currents flow.
Thoughts can change the brain's design
Attention draws the learning line.
The mind takes signals, small and deep,
from body's stir or gut's heartbeat,
then tunes to fields both wide and near Imagination,
insight, clear. It stands between the seen and dreamed,
where meaning forms and worlds are teamed.
The mind interprets what we find,
and makes the energy aligned.

The Universe: The Field of Connection

The universe is more than stars,
its patterns linking what we are.
A web of motion, thought, and light,
where everything affects the night.
In science and in ancient lore,
this field connects us evermore.
When thoughts and hearts are calm and kind,
they bring coherence to the mind.

The same design in star or cell,
in lung or wave, repeats as well.
From galaxies to drops of rain,
one geometry sustains the chain.
This universe, this boundless field,
Is where our minds and bodies yield.
We sense, we think, we co-create
One flow of life that integrates.

THE WIRES BENEATH THE WEATHER

A spark in the storm, a flicker, a flare, a mind on a tightrope, hung in the air. The highs burn bright, the lows run deep, in cycles that steal both wake and sleep.

Beneath the waves, the roots entwine, of nurture's wounds and nature's line. A code in the blood, a scar in the soul, each shapes the rhythm, but not the whole.

Childhood shadows that whisper and stay, teach the heart to hide or fray. When trust is broken before it's made, the colours of mood begin to fade.

The HPA hums its fractured tune, stress like thunder beneath the moon. Cortisol rises, the neurones spin, the storm begins to brew within.

Genes, like seeds in troubled ground, awake when trauma wraps around. In plastic minds they twist and bend, their melody altered by the end.

Emotion's reins grow worn and thin, hard to hold the storm within. From mania's peak to darkness' call, the fall feels endless if one should fall.

And yet through chaos, courage blooms, through trembling nights and silent rooms. For though the past may light the flame, it need not burn in endless shame.

With care and truth, with voice and art, we mend the wiring of the heart. For genes may hum and pain may scar, but healing proves how strong we are.

My Busy, Brilliant Mind

Sometimes my thoughts all spin and race, a thousand clouds across one space.
My mind won't stop, it hums all day, in its own bright and buzzing way.

I feel so much, all at one time, it's hard to name, to make it rhyme. But
feelings big don't mean I'm bad, they just show I care and that's not sad.

At school, it's tough the noise, the test, my brain won't pause, it needs a rest.
They say "just focus," but they don't see, how many worlds live inside of me.

Sometimes I'm tired, or scared, or small, sometimes I don't feel safe at all.
But deep inside, I know it's true, there's strength in thinking like I do.

My mind's not wrong, it's wired bright, it sees the dark and finds the light.
And though it's hard to slow or stay, I'm learning me in my own way.

So, if my heart feels loud or wild, that's just the song of this strange child.
I'll breathe, I'll rest, I'll take my time, this busy, brilliant brain is mine.

"I Spoke, But No One Heard"

I told them what he did to me the nights, the fear, the agony.
But calm deceit and practiced charm turned all my cries into false alarm.

He said my mind was "not quite sound," and all my truth came crashing down.
They called it stress; they called it spite; they made my pain his legal right.

They said I'd turned my child away, that love could twist and disobey. But all I did was try to keep my baby safe, my promise deep.

Each question cut, each gaze was cold, they stripped my story, piece by fold.
They took his mask for honesty and left me drowning silently.

They named my trauma “instability,”. My warning signs “hostility.” They dressed his violence up as care and called me mad for my despair.

But I am not the names they said. I am not the lies he fed.
I am the pulse that still remains the breath that rose through unseen chains.

Though courts may blind and justice sleep, I hold my truth, I hold it deep.
For every mother, bruised and scarred, still fighting systems built this hard.

We are the ones who still believe that truth is stronger than deceit. And one day, when the echoes fade, our voices will not be betrayed.

Rewrite, Rewire, Retrain

People don't change through facts on a page or wisdom that comes from a teacher or sage. For knowing the "how" is just part of the game, real change begins with who you became.

If deep down you whisper, "I always fail," Then every new habit is set to derail. No plan or new tool can truly defend, when your story insists how it all must end.

The mind holds tight to the self it once knew, protecting the old, though it no longer fits you. Even when misery knocks at your door, your subconscious says, "This is safer, no more."

So, seekers turn inward through breath-work and trance, through EMDR and hypnotic expanse. They dive for the root, the tale underneath, the script of the self we've woven in grief.

But stories alone don't keep us confined, it's the feeling that's welded the cage in the mind. The nerves say, "Stay here, it's what we know best," even if joy is a lifelong guest.

Your identity's laws, your own inner creed are written in feelings that planted the seed. Ten sacred commandments that whisper your part, not in your head, but deep in your heart. So don't just revisit the tales of your pain, change the emotion that keeps them the same.

Then teach your behaviour to follow anew, a story rewoven, alive, and true. To shift who you are takes more than the brain, you must rewrite, rewire, and finally retrain.

The Dance of Light and Shadow

The innocent dreams of peace so bright yet hides from storms, denies the night.
Their naïve side whispers, "Close your eyes,"
But truth still knocks, it never dies.

The Orphan longs where hearts belong,
seeks comfort deep when things go wrong.
Yet Victim sighs, "The world's unfair,"
forgets the strength that's always there.

The Hero fights with blazing flame,
to carve a path, to earn a name.
But when the Bully grips the sword,
they wound the weak, not save the world.

The Caregiver, gentle, soft, and true,
will give their heart to carry you.
But Martyr's chains can bleed the soul,
when saving others takes its toll.

The Explorer roams through endless skies,
seeks meaning where the horizon lies.
Yet Drifter's lost in restless spin,
afraid to land, to look within.

The Rebel breaks the walls of lies,
Brings fire where stale order dies.
But Destroyer, wild and blind,
burns the future, leaves none behind.

The Lover melts in passion's stream,
a tender heart, a sacred dream.
But Addict's grasp can drown the soul,
mistaking need for love's control.

The Creator shapes what none have seen,
dreams worlds from thought, pure and serene.
Yet Perfectionist, bound by fear,
destroys the art they hold so dear.

The Jester laughs at life's cruel game,
brings joy to hearts that know no name.
Yet Fool can hide behind the jest,
avoiding pain that shapes the best.

The Sage seeks truth in every word,
listens deeper than he's heard.
Yet Know-It-All, in lofty pride,
forgets that wisdom walks beside.

The Magician, bright and wise,
turns tears to stars before your eyes.
But Manipulator's dark delight,
bends truth to will and dims the light.

The Ruler builds with steady hand,
brings order, peace, and guides the land.
But Tyrant's fear of losing reign,
turns power sweet to bitter chain.

Each archetype, both dark and bright,
dances in our daily light.
The shadow's not a foe to fight,
but night that teaches what is right.

So, meet your mirror, name your pain in every loss, there's strength to gain.
For wholeness comes when all is known,
when light and dark stand not alone.

The Yawn Within

When tension winds the body tight, and thoughts race on through day and night, a whisper stirs, so soft, so wide
a yawn begins to open inside.

It isn't boredom's lazy tune, nor sleep that calls too soon, too soon, it's nature's sigh, a nervous balm, that brings the storming mind to calm.

The jaw expands, the lungs draw deep, the rhythm wakes from shallow sleep, the vagus hums, the circuits clear, the heart beats slow, the thoughts steer near.

One breath reshapes the inner skies, the restless fades, the balance lies. For in that stretch, that sacred yawn,
the system rights, the soul is drawn.

So when you feel your edges fray, and calm seems lost, just drift that way.
Let yawns unwind what's wound too tight,
and guide you gently back to right.

The Hidden Choir.

They told us five was all we knew, the senses five, the tried, the true. To see, to hear, to taste, to smell, to touch the world and that was well.

But deep inside, the body hums, a symphony of hidden drums. It knows its place, it feels its spin, it hears the pulse that beats within.

It feels the warmth, the ache, the time, it sings in rhythm, breath, and rhyme. It senses truth, and pain, and peace, the spaces where all words can cease.

It feels the heart of those nearby, it reads the silence, hears the sigh. It tastes the vibe, it feels the tone, it knows when souls are not alone.

You were not made to shut or hide, your sensing self is not denied. You're tuned to life to depth, to more, to whispers schools could not explore.

So breathe, remember, take it slow, ask softly what your body knows. You were never too sensitive no. You were simply built to feel the flow.

Let it return. Let it guide.
Let the truth live deep inside.
For what you sense is not untrue, it's the world remembering through you.

Made in the USA
Middletown, DE
15 November 2025

20875033R00051